A *Atheneum Books for Young Readers* • An imprint of Simon & Schuster Children's Publishing Division • 1230 Avenue of the Americas, New York, New York 10020 • Copyright © 2016 by Gilbert Ford • Photography by Greg Endries • All rights reserved, including the right of reproduction in whole or in part in any form. • ATHENEUM BOOKS FOR YOUNG READERS is a registered trademark of Simon & Schuster, Inc. • Atheneum logo is a trademark of Simon & Schuster, Inc. • For information about special discounts for bulk purchases, please contact Simon & Schuster Special Sales at 1-866-506-1949 or business @simonandschuster.com. • The Simon & Schuster Speakers Bureau can bring authors to your live event. For more information or to book an event, contact the Simon & Schuster Speakers Bureau at 1-866-248-3049 or visit our website at www.simonspeakers.com.

Jacket design by Lauren Rille and Gilbert Ford; interior design by Lauren Rille • The text for this book was set in Neutra. • The illustrations for this book were drawn and colored digitally and then printed, assembled with found objects into dioramas, and photographed. • Manufactured in China • 0717 SCP • 10 9 8 7 6 5 4 3 • Library of Congress Cataloging-in-Publication Data • Ford, Gilbert. • The marvelous thing that came from a spring : the accidental invention of the toy that swept the nation / by Gilbert Ford. • pages cm • Audience: Ages 4-8. • Audience: K to grade 3. • ISBN 978-1-4814-5065-2 (hardcover) • ISBN 978-1-4814-5066-9 (eBook) • 1. Slinky (Toy) 2. James, Richard T., 1914-1974. 3. James, Betty, 1918-2008. 4. Inventors—United States—Biography. I. Title. •GV1218.5.F67 2016 • 790.133dc23 • 2015015309

To Leo:
may your life be filled with invention and *play*

written and illustrated by
Gilbert Ford

photography by
Greg Endries

The MARVELOUS THING THAT CAME FROM A SPRING

The Accidental Invention of the Toy That Swept the Nation

Atheneum Books for Young Readers
New York London Toronto Sydney New Delhi

ichard James was a dreamer. But in 1943 the United States was at war. Richard had to support his country and his family, so he worked as an engineer for the United States Navy in a shipyard in Philadelphia. His assignment was to invent a device that would keep fragile ship equipment from vibrating in choppy seas.

Richard tried all kinds of springs, but nothing was working. Then one day a torsion spring fell from the shelf above his desk. Its coils took a walk . . .

and so did Richard's imagination.

This spring might not work for the navy's ships—but Richard knew he had stumbled onto something. What was it?

After work Richard rushed home
and showed his wife, Betty, the floppy spring.

They gave the spring to their son Tom,
who let it go from the top of the stairs.

The family watched in astonishment as it . . .

walked all the way down!

"I think it's a toy!" Richard marveled. Betty thought so too. She also thought that if they wanted to share their discovery with the world, they needed to figure out what on Earth to call the thing!

Betty thumbed through a dictionary for two days, underlining words.
Nothing sounded quite right . . . until she found "slinky," meaning
"graceful" and "curvy in movement." "Slinky" also sounded like the swish
and clink of the spring's coils in motion.

It was only a name, but it was just right. With one word, Betty thought she could transform this spring:

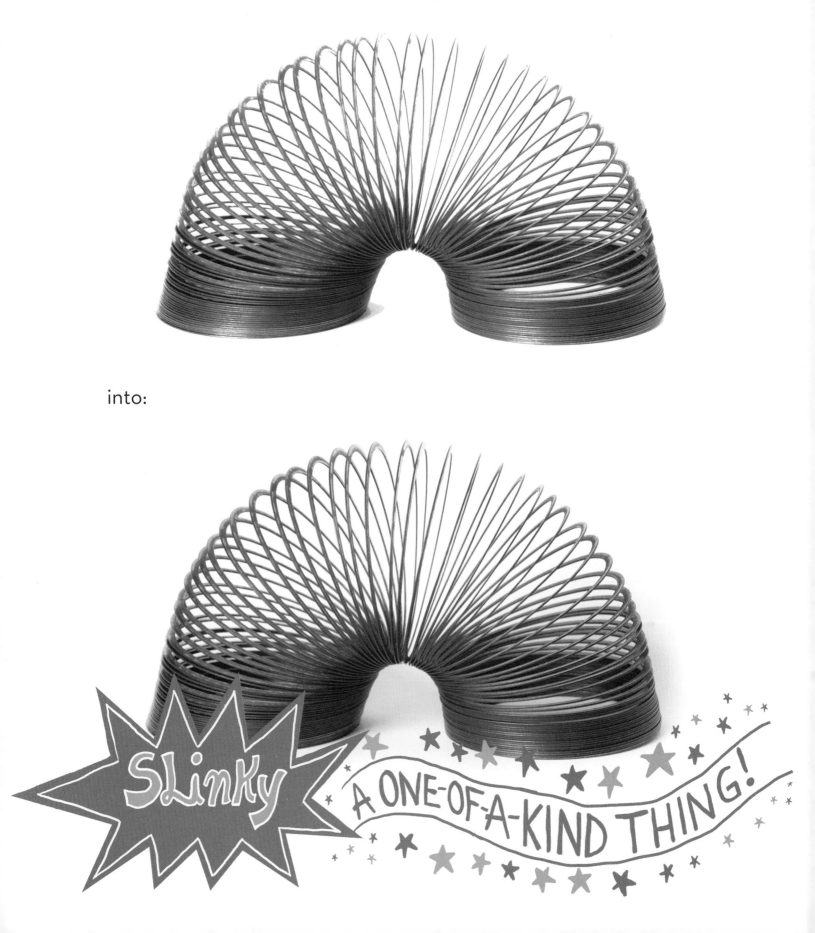

into:

Slinky

A ONE-OF-A-KIND THING!

Richard and Betty wanted to produce a lot of Slinkys, but they did not have the money to do it. So Richard sprang for the bank and took out a five-hundred-dollar loan to have four hundred Slinkys made.

Once they arrived, Richard brought his invention to every toy store in Philadelphia—but no one wanted it.

Was the Jameses' idea a flop?

Finally, he tried a large department store called Gimbels. Gimbels showed as little interest in the toy as the other stores, but Richard begged the manager to allow him to demonstrate how it worked to the holiday shoppers. Just once.

And so, on a stormy night in November 1945, with Christmas just weeks away, shoppers poured into Gimbels. They were searching for the next great stocking stuffer—and Richard was ready.

He placed the coil at the top of the ramp he had built and scanned the store for Betty.

Where was she?

Betty was still pacing back and forth at home. She was afraid no one would want the toy.

Just in case, she asked her friend to pose as an excited shopper and gave her a dollar to buy one.

But Richard was unable to wait any longer.
So he took a deep breath and let the Slinky go.

When Betty finally arrived at Gimbels, there was no need to pretend to love the toy—all four hundred Slinkys had sold in ninety minutes.

The Slinky was a hit!

* SLiNKY *
Sold OUT!

16

The war ended that same year, and the troops returned home to marry their sweethearts. A baby boom soon followed, and demand for the Slinky skyrocketed.

So Richard dreamed up an even bigger idea. He used his engineering skills to build a machine that could coil eighty feet of steel wire into a Slinky in ten seconds.

While Richard made the Slinkys and drove the delivery van, Betty kept the business running smoothly. She frantically filled orders, sent and collected payments . . .

and hid their profits in a roasting pan below the basement!

Soon, there was more business than the Jameses
could handle by themselves.

So Richard and Betty built a factory and hired twenty people to work for them.

At last, they were able to spin out enough Slinkys for every child in America to have one.

Today, the Slinky still inspires kids—of all ages, and all across the globe—to *play*.

It took the teamwork of a dreamer and a planner to turn an ordinary spring . . .

The Slinky walked its way across the cultural landscape in 1945 and has kept walking ever since. Even though it was originally intended as a toy, it has sparked people to invent different uses for it. The Slinky was used as an antenna for radios during the Vietnam War, as a device for understanding wave mechanics, and as a therapy tool for patients who had suffered from strokes or other disorders. It was launched into space on the shuttle *Discovery* to help astronauts demonstrate how gravity worked. And the clinking coils of the Slinky even inspired a musician, John Cage, to create experimental music based on the sound!

In 1960, Richard James, still the dreamer, left to do missionary work in Bolivia. With James Industries nearly bankrupt, Betty took over and relocated the factory to Hollidaysburg, Pennsylvania.

Within four years, under her leadership, the company sprang back to life! Betty expanded the line and advertised the Slinky on TV. The famous jingle is still remembered today:

"What walks down stairs, alone or in pairs, and makes a slinkity sound? A spring, a spring, a marvelous thing. Everyone knows it's Slinky. . . ."

Today, Slinky is still made in the United States. More than 250 million of the toys have been produced since its invention, by machines based on Richard James's original design.

In 2001, Betty James was inducted into the Toy Industry Hall of Fame.

THANKS

I would like to thank Betsy Partridge, for her guidance as I wrote my first nonfiction picture book. Thanks to my agent, Steve Malk, for reading over my early mock-ups and offering suggestions—even pushing me to try it in a different style. A special thanks goes to my editor, Emma Ledbetter, and my art director, Lauren Rille, for helping me make this book the best it could be. Thanks to my brother, Drew, for assisting me with the setups on a day's notice. Thank you to Dan Treiber from dansparentshouse.com, for allowing me to dig through his basement for objects. Thanks to my grandmother Betty Ford, for never throwing anything away. And last, a big thank-you to Greg Endries, who tirelessly photographed my models—even after the fifth redo.

BIBLIO

Harry, Lou. *It's Slinky: The Fun and Wonderful Toy*. Philadelphia: Running Press, 2000.

Ikenson, Ben. *Patents: Ingenious Inventions: How They Work and How They Came to Be*. New York: Black Dog & Leventhal Publishers, 2004.

Jones, Charlotte Foltz. *Mistakes That Worked*. New York: Doubleday, 1991.

Wulffson, Don. *Toys!: Amazing Stories Behind Some Great Inventions*. New York: Henry Holt, 2000.